Meet the
Sherpas

by Lisa Moore

SCHOOL PUBLISHERS

Cover, ©Alison Wright/CORBIS; p.5, ©Sheldan Collins/CORBIS; p.4-5, ©Rob Howard/CORBIS; p.6, ©James Burke/Time Life Pictures/Getty Images; p.7, ©DEVENDRA M SINGH/AFP/Getty Images; p.8, ©Michael S. Lewis/CORBIS; p.9, ©PunchStock; p.10, ©PAWEL KOPCZYNSKI/Reuters/CORBIS; p.11, ©Design Pics/PunchStock; p.12, ©CORBIS; p.14, ©David Samuel Robbins/Stone/Getty Images.

Printed in Hong Kong

ISBN 10: 0-15-351047-1
ISBN 13: 978-0-15-351047-2

Ordering Options
ISBN 10: 0-15-350602-4 (Grade 5 On-Level Collection)
ISBN 13: 978-0-15-350602-4 (Grade 5 On-Level Collection)
ISBN 10: 0-15-357972-2 (package of 5)
ISBN 13: 978-0-15-357972-1 (package of 5)

4 5 6 7 8 9 10   0940   12 11 10 09

Today a group of people called Sherpas live near the summit of Mount Everest. Mount Everest is the highest mountain in the world. It is in the country of Nepal, which is located between India and China in Asia.

Americans say "Sherpa," but in Nepal, they say "Sharwa." *Shar* means east and *wa* means person, so the name means "people from the east." For generations, Sherpas have lived in and climbed the great Himalaya mountains. As a result, they have become acclimated to the high altitudes.

There are about 100,000 Sherpas in the world today. About 35,000 of them live in the valley on the southern side of Mount Everest. Some also live in India, Bhutan, and Tibet, a region of China. Thousands of other Sherpas live in Europe and North America.

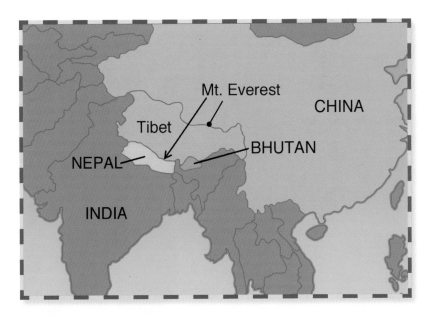

Sherpas are born into one of eighteen clans, or extended families. They call these groups *ru*. All eighteen *ru* are equal. Many Sherpas use their clan name as their last name. Traditionally, each Sherpa marries someone from outside his or her *ru*.

Many Sherpas name their children after the day of the week on which they were born. Here is a chart of the days of the week in the Sherpa language.

Sunday	*Nima*
Monday	*Dawa*
Tuesday	*Mingma*
Wednesday	*Lhakpa*
Thursday	*Phurba*
Friday	*Pasanag*
Saturday	*Pemba*

Sherpas are accustomed to producing their own food and clothing. Most families herd big animals called yaks. Yaks give them wool for clothing and leather for shoes. They even burn yak droppings for fuel! They use yak milk to make butter and cheese.

Sherpas also farm. Most families have a garden, and many make their living from farming. One of their main dishes is *shyakpa*, a meat and potato stew with vegetables. They also eat *daal bhaat*, made of rice and lentils. Tea is the favorite drink. Most Sherpas like it with lots of milk and sugar.

The most famous Sherpa of all was probably Tenzing Norgay. On May 29, 1953, Tenzing guided Sir Edmund Hillary of New Zealand and his team to the top of Mount Everest. They became the first humans to reach the summit. In some ways, their climb changed the Sherpa world forever. After it, visitors from all over the world began to pour into Nepal to climb its peaks. Sherpas like Tenzing became their guides.

Sir Edmund Hillary and Tenzing Norgay

Lhakpa Sherpa became the first woman to reach the summit for a third time in 2003. She was accompanied by her brother and her fifteen-year-old sister, Ming Kipa Sherpa. Ming became the youngest person ever to climb Mount Everest.

Lhakpa Sherpa and her brother, Mingma

The Sherpa language is spoken, not written. In schools today, most Sherpas learn to read, write, and speak Nepali. Some, who go to Buddhist schools, also read and write Tibetan. Sherpas in India speak English and Hindi. Of course, Sherpas who work in the hiking business often speak English, German, French, Italian, and other languages so that they can speak to their customers.

A Handful of Sherpa Words

far away	*thakringbu*	moon	*dawa*
to climb	*zeku*	tea	*solja*
it is snowing	*ka gepsung*	potatoes	*riggi*
sunshine	*nima sharsung*	music	*lu*
sun	*nam*		

If you visit the home of a Sherpa, you should know about *shey-sa*, their word for respect and politeness. The custom is for the guest to refuse food or drink until it has been offered three times. Then, the guest may accept. In a Sherpa home, a guest should never ask for more food during a meal. The host will offer food to guests all around until the meal is finished. Don't forget to say, "No, thank you" the first two times food is offered. That way, you'll show that you understand the custom of *shey-sa*.

The small villages of the Sherpa region called Khumbu are a world of steep cliffs and jagged rocks. There are no paved roads. There are no motor vehicles. There are no telephones. There is no electricity. Most houses are wooden and humble. One reporter from *National Geographic* described them as perched on the sides of steep hills "like colorful [building] blocks."

Because of the steep hillsides, farmers plow their land into flat areas called terraces. These flat steps keep any water flowing down the mountains from washing away seeds and soil.

Schools are new to Sherpas. Until recently, the only Sherpas who went to school were studying to become Buddhist priests. Before this century, Sherpa girls never went to school. The first public schools were built in the 1960s, but there are high schools in only a few villages. Sir Edmund Hillary, who believed that education was essential, funded some of the schools. To build them, he established a special fund. This money has also helped build hospitals and clinics in Nepal.

Today, many hiking companies and other businesses are owned by young Sherpas. They have new, modern ways that must seem strange to their parents. For many Sherpas, the new ways are in collision with the old ways. To succeed in the modern business world, young Sherpas must know how to speak to foreigners, keep budgets, and negotiate contracts.

Bandinima Sherpa was a student at one of Hillary's schools in Pangmo. Today, she is the first woman vice president of the Trekking Agents Association of Nepal. (*Trekking* is another word for hiking in the mountains.) Her job is to make sure that *all* workers in the trekking business get fair treatment. Porters, teashop owners, guides, and trash collectors each deserve a share of the profits. A hiker herself, she has led groups to the far corners of Nepal and Tibet. Bandinima Sherpa is a good example of a modern Sherpa who bridges the cultures of the east and west.

Today more than half of all Sherpas make their living serving tourists. With earnings of $2,000 a year or more in a country where the average yearly income is less than $175, Sherpa cooks, guides and camp staff are among the best paid people in Nepal.

About one hundred Sherpas have reached the summit of Everest. One of them, Appa Sherpa, has made it sixteen times. In 1991, an all-Sherpa team climbed Everest.

"This is our expedition," said one team member. "It is for all the Sherpas."

Here are some lines from a Sherpa poem that has been translated into English. As you read the lines aloud, picture jagged, snowy peaks. Picture climbers like little red and yellow dots, far away on the thin trails. Imagine the smells of potato stew and sweet hot tea. Imagine the Sherpas singing to you, inviting you to visit their land.

I wait for you day after day,
where the grass is high and
the flowers are sweet.
Someday we will meet.
I wait for you where
the rocks are singing.
I wait for you where
the air is shimmering.
I wait for you where
the moon is shining.
I wait for you where
the birds are singing.
I wait for you where the sun is warmest.
I wait for you in spring
when the sun is shining longer.
I wait for you;
the winter has already gone.

Like many native people, Sherpas are tugged between the old ways of their ancestors and the new ways of the modern world. As more and more tourists visit their towns and villages, young people learn the ways of the visitors and question the ways of their parents. More and more study in other countries and travel to other parts of the world. Many of the Sherpa traditions remain secure, however. Perhaps it is because some of the old ways are the best ways. Perhaps it is because tourists love to experience the old ways. Perhaps it is because the mountains, especially Mount Everest, are a constant reminder of their past.

Think Critically

1. What event led to the biggest change in Sherpa culture in the twentieth century?

2 List three facts about Sherpas that you learned from this book. Then, list two opinions that you read.

3 What does this book suggest about the traditions of native people?

4 What do you think of the Sherpa tradition of *shey-sa*? How do you think it came to be?

5 Based on this book, what are three words you would use to describe Sherpas?

 Science

Nepal and Tibet Do research on the Internet or using other library resources to learn about how and when the Himalayas were formed. Make and illustrate a poster to display your findings.

School-Home Connection At home, try to create the feel of a Sherpa meal. If possible, cook a version of either shyakpa or daal bhaat. Serve sweet tea with milk. Practice some form of shey-sa. Be sure to explain to your family and friends what you are doing and why!